Nahant

ACCOUNTS OF UNEXPLAINED OCCURRENCES IN NAHANT, MASSACHUSETTS

By Gerald W. Butler, Captain, MSG, Ret.

Nahauntus
Accounts of Unexplained Occurrences in Nahant, Massachusetts

Author: Gerald Butler, Captain, MSG, Retired, SFH

Original Illustrations by: Gerald W. Butler

A note on spelling: For stylistic reasons and those of internal consistency, often the text retains the older English spelling of specific words, such as "covern" for "coven," and "devill" for "devil."

We founded f/64 Publishing to promote crisp, clear storytelling that captures those details essential to understanding a subject. Like making a photographic exposure at f/64, this takes time and strategy…and can result in breathtaking work. The company is also named partly in honor of the association of photographers co-founded by Ansel Adams: Group f.64.

---

f/64 Publishing
Portland, Maine
www.f64publishing.com
www.f64publishing.com

ISBN: 978-0-9831858-5-7
Written and Published in the USA

f/64 Publishing

To my daughters Heather, Tara, and Alanna, my son Michael,
my grandchildren Emily, Sara, Parker, Aiden, and Amelia,
and my parents Mr. and Mrs. Gerald F. Butler, of Nahant

**It is a thing of no great difficulty to
raise objections against another man's
oration; nay, it is an easy matter.
But to produce a better in its place is a
work extremely troublesome.**

Plutarch, c. 46 - c. 120

Contents

Acknowledgments

We are grateful for the assistance of:

Tara Maureen Butler
Heather Ann Butler - Cook
Alanna May Butler - Guptill
Lynn Nahant Historical Society
Nahant Public Library
Right Reverend Arch Priestess, Temple of Ancient Wisdom, Llaluna Pellegrina
Reverend Madelein Swart, Crooked Crow Covern, Capetown, South Africa
United States Army
United States Coast Guard
Diane L. Ward

Image Contributions:

ALB - Alanna May Butler-Guptill
CDG - United States Coast Guard
DAV - David Morin
EAP - Emily Ann Pauli
HAC - Heather Ann Butler-Cook
LPL - Lynn Public Library
NHS - Nahant Historical Society
PUB - Public Domain
PWC - Parker William Cook
RNA - H. M. Royal Navy Archives
SEC - Sarah Elizabeth Cook
SHS - Salem Historical Society
TMB - Tara Maureen Butler
UNK - Unkown
USA - Unites States Army

Chapter One

Thorvald the Norseman

While many townships and countries claim the burial ground for the explorer Thorvald, numerous documents and books put his final resting place on our New England shores, including claims that he was laid to rest in Nahant, Massachusetts.

The township of Nahant is extremely small, and in fact is the smallest in all of the Commonwealth of Massachusetts. The tiny town juts into Massachusetts Bay and was considered an island until a sturdy causeway was built in recent times. Now recognized as a peninsula, the scenic town has one of the most beautiful settings for enjoying clean, fresh air off the Atlantic, picturesque cliffs and beaches, and the most astounding sunrises and sunset locales. It also boasts extraordinary tales of mystery and intrigue, occult occurrences and paranormal activity.

Our first legend involves Thorvald the Viking.

Thorvald

In a much earlier time, Nahant belonged to Lynn, under the majestic umbrella of the Royal British Empire. Before the New England area was colonized, other explorers visited. Some explorers were welcomed by the Native Americans, although some natives and tribes were entirely eliminated by the New World explorers' common diseases and warlike nature.

Enter Thorvald... On his Third Voyage, Thorvald, the son of Eirek the Red and brother of Leif Eriksson,

A striking ink rendering of a Viking warrior in battle dress from an old print. *PUB*

reportedly visited what is now known as Nahant, in 1004. The area was recognized as *Krassones,* also being spelled *Krossness.* Later, the area was also reportedly visited by Gosnold. Many years later, in an address by Senator Henry Cabot Lodge, Nahant's premier statesman, Lodge said, "...but we have fair ground to suppose that Thorvald, one of the old Norse fighters, lies buried in Nahant." Further speculative research indicates that the area Thorvald's warcraft anchored was between Bayley's Hill and the present town wharf while his burial site may have been atop Bayley's Hill, which is now recognized as Bailey's Hill.

Thorvald was reportedly the first European to set foot on Nahant. In 1004, he sailed from Eiriksfjord Greenland to investigate Vinland, located in the southern areas. He then sailed to Leifsbudir (Leif's Huts) now believed to have been located at L'Anse aux Meadows, Newfoundland, using the known Norse se route, where his brother, Leif, had wintered the previous year. Using that as a base he then sailed farther south until damage from pounding waves to his vessel required repair.

He put his vessel into a densely wooded promontory, identified later as being Nahant. Thorvald named his place *Kjalarnes*, or *Keelness*. Taken aback by the beautiful setting - believed to be Bayley's Hill - he stated: "Here it is beautiful, and here would I like to raise my dwelling." Although it was a breathtaking area, it was also considered a savage place; infested by wolves, bears and other wild beasts.

Large fires were lit, made from driftwood and fallen trees, and were used for protection and illumination. Simultaneously, guards were posted throughout the time of darkness. In the day time a solitary guard patrolled the landward area of their encampment, alternating with members of the keel working crew.

A typical, fully manned Norseman war craft under sail. From an old print. *PUB*

The tragic death of Theovald Erikson. Art taken from an old print. *PUB*

Fresh water was available nearby and wild animals were slain to survive. A crude lean-to was created to protect the men against inclement weather and to provide for sleep in comfort and safety. After repairs to the boat's keel were completed, the explorers encountered nine Native Americans, or *Skraelings,* the Norse term for the natives.

The natives, hidden in the thick forest, secretly watched the explorers repair their large canoe and became curious. A small number of the natives slowly came out of hiding and attempted to talk with the Norsemen. All met in a peaceful but guarded manner. Unfortunately, friendly discussion quickly turned into an argument, probably due to misunderstanding of the speech communication and hand gestures.

Within a very short time tempers flared and hostilities ensued. This resulted in eight of the nine natives being killed, while one native managed to escape. He returned later that afternoon with a large war-party intent on slaying the Norsemen.

During the fierce battle that followed, the *Skraelings* launched a barrage of arrows against the Norsemen. Thorvald ordered his men aboard ship and had the battle screens raised to protect his men.

When the natives exhausted their supply of arrows, they quickly melted into the dense woods nearby. Thorvald asked his men if there was anyone wounded from the battle and they replied no.

He then told his men that he had received a well-placed arrow that had found its way between the battle screen of the ship and his personal shield, piercing him under his arm, striking a mortal blow.

The natives soon returned and launched another barrage of arrows at the ship, but the Norsemen, overcome by fury at the coming loss of Thorvald, jumped off the ship, onto the ground and engaged the natives, completely and savagely annihilating their entire war party.

Thorvald, mortally wounded, commanded his men to quickly depart. His order, as passed down through

A representation of a fierce Native American warrior of the New England Tribe in Massachusetts. *GWB*

history, stated: "I now advise you to prepare for your departure as soone as possible; but me ye shall bring to the promontory where I thought it good to dwell. There ye shall bury me; and plant a cross at my head and also at my feet, and call the place Krossanes in all times coming."

Thorvald's last boon was to have Kjalarnes renamed Krossaness (Cross Cape) which was done immediately. The Norsemen quickly departed and returned to *Leifsbudit* to stay the winter. In the spring they sailed to *Eiriksford.*

A number of historians document *Krossanes* as being Nahant with further speculation that Thorvald's burial site lay atop what we now call Bayley's Hill.

Following the departure of the Norsemen, the natives returned to the site where their fighters had been killed and gave them ritual burials.

The large crosses that marked Thorvald's burial were pushed over and set afire, while the grave site of Thorvald was unearthed and his remains were completely and savagely demolished. His dismembered

Bayley's Hill as seen from Pond Beach, c. late-1800s. *PUB*

body was cursed and defiled by the natives and left for wild animals to devour, while the natives regarded the site as evil and unclean and did not visit for many years.

In the following centuries the area was deforested and the wild beasts were removed, making it a safe grazing area for farmers and livestock. Rumors of the period gave credence that Thorvald's grave was protected by evil wolves, bears and spirits. The most creditable were that avenging Norsemen made fire to prepare to find those that killed their leader and to torture the men that defiled his grave. The tales eventually waned and were mostly forgotten.

Henry Wadsworth Longfellow, who summered in Nahant, was another who believed that the Vikings had visited New England, and illuminated his thoughts in a number of his poems.

Regardless, further evidence of the site of Krossaness, the remains of Thorvald, or the presence on that journey of his Norsemen, have yet to be officially discovered.

In years to follow, during various seasons, a small glowing aura in a subdued shade of cold blue was viewed atop Bayley's Hill. It was an arctic glow that lasted briefly. In most instances, the glow was ex lained as being derived from a group of merrymakers quaffing beer and ale, using driftwood to keep varm.

Dying campfire embers were also considered a primary cause of the glow while later explanations suggested a pocket of natural gas. The light was infrequent and not viewed from a distance. There was no noise, nd contrary to the theory of campfire embers, no burn marks or ashes left behind, nor was anyone seen ntering or leaving the hill during or after the sightings.

There was absolutely no evidence of its cause, or lingering evidence of it truly existing.

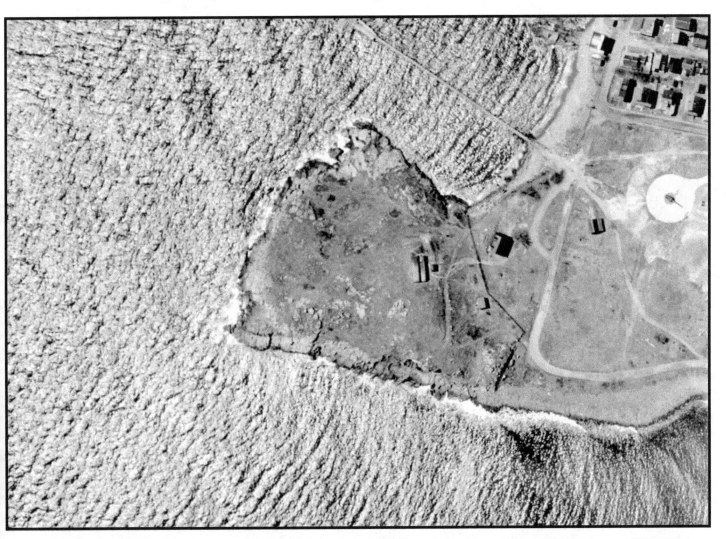

A remarkable aerial image of Bayley's Hill showing site and military installations, c. 1924. *USA*

Chapter Two

Bayley's Hill

Enter the ice-blue aura... The aura sightings became less frequent as Bayley's Hill became known as a tranquil and beautiful location to view the sea and sky and observe the sailing ships plying the coastal waters. In 1875, the Tudor family purchased most of Bayley's Hill and built a very comfortable residence. Later the hill was owned by other parties and a hotel was constructed on its lower segment.

During the Spanish American War, the hill was manned by soldiers, artillerymen, and military electrical engineers. Tents were set and equipment was placed to control a minefield at the entrance to Lynn Harbor. Two rapid-fire guns were also emplaced on the hill. On the evening prior to the small garrison leaving, an ice-blue aura appeared not far from the gun emplacements. It quickly waned. The area was investigated thoroughly as ammunition was stored in the vicinity. Nothing was discovered--no embers, nor residual burns on the ground. The incident was passed over as a nocturnal fantasy. After the soldiers departed the site little mention was made of lights on Bayleys Hill.

In 1906, the United States Army began construction of a modern Observation Station on the military crest of Bayley's Hill. The sweep of view was majestic from this point and the military took full advantage using it for observation and to direct fire upon enemy warcraft if they attempted to enter the Port of Boston.

During construction, the United States Engineer Department did not make note of any ancient timber remnants found during excavation of the observation station nor were bones unearthed. When the natives desecrated and demolished the grave site of Thorvald, the timbers were probably completely burned, wild beasts eliminated any remnants of his shredded body, and his personal armor was taken as pillage trophies.

The observation station was completed and intermittently manned from 1907 through January 1915, when a powerful searchlight had been proposed and built into the hill's cliff. Additionally, they con-

Bayley's Hill, distant center, capturing the general area of the burial site. *NHS*

U. S. Army Observation and Range Finding station at Bayley's Hill, c. 1924. *USA*

Bayley's Hill 60-inch searchlight unit shown in its operating position, c. 1924. *USA*

A low tide, water-level image of Bayley's Hill captured from Bass Point, c. 2012. *TMB*

The western lower area of Bayley's Hill facing the town wharf in the distance, c. 2015. *EAP*

structed a power station to supply electrical power to both the searchlight and the observation station. Reserve militia units manned the stations at varying times for training and as World War I loomed, the sites were constantly manned due to threat of a German invasion of Boston and the Cape Cod area.

Fortunately, this never occurred, but the ice-blue aura was randomly observed at the top of the hill, near the observation station. Initially thought to be a soldier with a cigarette or a small fire to keep warm, soldiers of the guard found nothing upon investigation of the area. To find an explanation for the apparition, officers concluded that the glow was probably a reflection of the searchlight off the water or a cloud and a patch of snow or ice on the ground.

That was understandable during a portion of the winter, but when a sighting took place in spring of that year, the officers and men were perplexed. It was passed on as a natural phenomenon. During the infamous "Bass Point Fire," soldiers protecting the massive gun battery noticed a faint glow near the observation station. Soldiers were immediately sent to extinguish the small fire but when they arrived, no fire or smoldering embers were found.

It was decided that all embers from the suspected conflagration had burned themselves out. After the situation was under control and it became light, a few soldiers walked up to the observation station for fresh air. Out of curiosity, one of them, who had been part of the detail sent during the night, thoroughly re-investigated the area trying to find a burnt spot. Out of curiosity, the other soldiers joined in the search. Nothing was found.

Years passed, and in 1940, elements of coast artillery personnel were garrisoned in what was then recognized as Fort Ruckman. Tents were set in martial rows below Bayleys Hill while officers were quartered in the observation station. Twice, an aura was observed on the hill at night, and once again, under investigation, nothing was found. At dawn the area was repeatedly inspected thoroughly. Nothing abnormal was found.

At the early part of World War II, Fort Ruckman was garrisoned to its maximum capacity with soldiers, barracks, tents and equipment. The threat of German submarines and enemy commandos attacking forts in the Boston harbor was quite real. Soldiers on guard duty and patrol were armed and conditioned to fire upon

Prewar soldiers atop Bayley's Hill. *GWB*

anyone who did not reply favorably to a password. In 1942, during a summer's eve, a sentinel on Bayley's Hill noticed a small glow near the observation station.

The coastline and seaward area were under extremely strict blackout conditions, so the soldier began to walk over to investigate. The glow slowly extinguished. Thinking it might be an officer having a cigarette, he prepared himself as how to address an officer breaking a wartime regulation.

As he walked closer, another glow appeared, but smaller. Within seconds, additional lights appeared and the soldier asked for a password. No password was returned. The soldier again asked for the password, but again no answer was audible. After asking the third time and receiving silence in return, the soldier cocked and fired his rifle into the midst of lights.

The result was electric. Sirens at Fort Ruckman blared, troops rushed out of barracks and climbed aboard troop trucks, and directed by Sergeants, went to the edge of the reservation's boundaries and beaches to either engage an unknown enemy or wait. Searchlight crews swept the immediate waters near Bayley's Hill while simultaneously the Harbor Defense Headquarters at Fort Banks was notified.

Enlisted members of the Fort Ruckman garrison reacting to the "fire-fly" incident, c. 1942. *GWB*

Within minutes the entirety of the Boston Harbor Defense Network was alert and ablaze with powerful searchlights sweeping the water and sky. The Sergeant of the Guard and Officer of the Day (OD) at Nahant questioned the soldier who fired his rifle as the area was quickly enveloped by combat-ready soldiers. A complete search of every area atop Bayley's Hill ensued. No enemy saboteurs or soldiers were found, no tracks of aggressors were discovered. It was a mystery.

As the soldier hurriedly explained his circumstances, the lights began to slowly appear once more, the soldiers, in unison, all brought their weapons to bear. One private, who formerly resided in the deep south, yelled to his Sergeant, "Sergent, them ain't soldiers with flashlights...them are firefly's!"

Thus ended a very tense situation with both laughter and great relief. No glow or lights were reported until early 1960. One of the Nike missile duty sergeants noticed a glow near the outside fence on Bayley's Hill near the radars. The Nike-Ajax missile sites were prime targets for saboteurs and the sergeant became duly alarmed. He immediately notified the Sergeant of the Guard who sounded the alarm and ordered armed troops to the spot. This required soldiers to go to the arms room, obtain rifles and ammunition, and climb around the exterior fence overlooking Lewis Beach to assemble near the waiting sergeant.

M. Emily Cook-Pauli at the general location of the "energy core" atop Bayley's Hill, c. 2019. *HAC*

By the time the soldiers arrived and were directed to the spot, the aura had extinguished itself. The alarm terminated, though armed soldiers patrolled the area during the remainder of the night. The next morning the sergeant formed another detail to thoroughly investigate the sighting area, but once again nothing was discovered.

Never has the military explained the strange ice-blue aura or glow on Bayley's Hill. If Thorvald had been vanquished at this spot and desecrated by native warriors, it could be his spirit, or it could yet be a natural phenomenon that only occurs rarely. There have been no military-related reports of this glow since 1960, though local theories abound. The more interesting ones pertain to Wica...

Chapter Three

Wicca

Enter an old religion at a new time... In the early 1980s, superficial evidence of ground circles began to appear on Bayley's Hill. It soon became suspected as evidence of an occult religion called Wicca. Wicca is a present day Paganistic religion using rituals and exercises, herbs and nature, encompassed within a vast ethical code. It also celebrates the solstices and equinoxes under the guidance of a female goddess, known as Mother Goddess, and a male god recognized as the Horned God.

Considered a present-day application of pre-Christian beliefs and practices, Wicca is founded upon ancient rituals and practiced by individuals or groups, known as Covens. Similar with Druidism in its environmental basis, Wicca is regarded as the inspiration of the spiritual goddess movement. Rituals include holidays focused upon phases of the moon; solar equinoxes and solstices, with elements of fire, water, air and earth; and emotional ceremonial initiations.

Mr. Gerald Gardner, an Englishman, is considered the founder of the Gardnerian tradition, a modern sect of Wicca as he learned and came to practice it in the 1960s. He wrote in his book "The Meaning of Witchcraft" (1959) that he word "witch" was derived from the Saxon word "Wica" that means "Wise People." While he seemed to use the word "wica" as the singular noun for a practitioner of the ancient ways, and there are variant spellings, the religion's modern accepted spelling is "Wicca" and practitioners are called "Wiccan" or "Wiccans."

Traditional British Wicca, especially as promoted by Gardner and his devotee Alex Sanders (who founded the Alexandrian Wicca tradition), is the basis for much of North American Wicca. Though some North American Pagan Witchcraft sects reject the term Wicca, such as within the Dianic tradition, the term

"The Pentacle is a symbol of a star enclosed in a circle. The upward point of the star represents the spirit. The other four points all represent an element: earth, air, fire and water. All of these things contribute to life and are part of each of us." - Unknown author, from the article "The Symbolic Meaning of the Pentagram" Image by *GWB*

Wicca broadly applies to North American pagan traditions that were heavily influenced by Gardner, Sanders, and contemporary twentieth century Englishmen.

The religion embraces those who enjoy the aura of nature itself. For example, watching a sunrise or sunset, observing the ocean in all its moods, absorbing the beauty of a moon-lit night, observing the first rays of daylight in the mountains, the desert, a meadow or the sea. The sun warming your face, colorful leaves in Autumn, and the light, dark and grey shadows of all in between.

There is much more to this religion. Wicca may be traced back to the Paleolithic period when followers worshiped a Fertile Goddess and a Horned God.

Primitive cave wall paintings illustrate a male form with the head of a stag standing outside a circle with a pregnant woman standing in the middle of a circle and eleven others surrounding.

Years later such a group would be termed a Coven, which consists often of thirteen male and female members. Although in process of resurrection, the Goddess and Horned God of Wicca predate Christianity by 28,000 years!

A Wiccan Coven encirclement celebrating joy, nature and oneness. *GWB*

A striking capture of a Wiccan Goddess preparing to cast white spells. *GWB*

The strict *Code for Wiccans* is recognized as the *Law of Three*. This irrevocable law means that "whatever we send out into our world shall return to us threefold, either benevolent or malevolent. A true Witch of Wicca would hesitate to create magick to manipulate or harm another, because of the Law of Three. In present day vernacular, the Law of Three may be interpreted as, "What goes around, comes around..."

Wiccans cast white spells in order to create favorable changes. This usually consists of members of a Coven who create and surround a sacred circle to make invocations to the guardians of the cardinal compass points. Certain candles and incense would be situated at varying points and places. At this point, the Coven would sit and relax both mind and body. Part of the ritual consists of the High Priestess standing inside the Sacred Circle with a gap in the Northeast sector. The circle is used because of its impregnable manner and significance. The most accurate description of a Sacred Circle is from a post in The Temple of Ancient Wisdom:

In the circle, we are all equal.
There is no one in front of you,

A Wiccan woman enjoying solitude and peace from within on Nahant's cliffs. *GWB*

and there's nobody behind you,
No one is above you,
No one is below you.
The circle is sacred because,
it was designed to create unity.

Once the Sacred Circle has been properly established, the remainder of the Coven stands outside the circle, and the ritual begins with a chant:

Black spirits and white,
Red spirits and gray,
Harken to the rune I say.
Four points of the Circle, weave the spell,
East, South, West, North, your tale tell.
East break of day,

South is white for the noontide hour,
In the West is twilight gray,
And North is black, for the place of power.
Three times round the Circle's cast.
Great ones, spirits from the past,
Witness it and guard it fast.

Following the healing or purpose of celebration, the ritual is completed, the circle is terminated, and the Coven dismissed.

Bayley's Hill has been mentioned many times as being a "spark spot," or a "spiritual crossroads." Where the spiritual crossroads meet is called a "dynamo" or "energy center." The generally accepted terminology for a "dynamo" is Vortice. Vortices are connected to other Vortices by Ley Lines. Within the Greater Boston

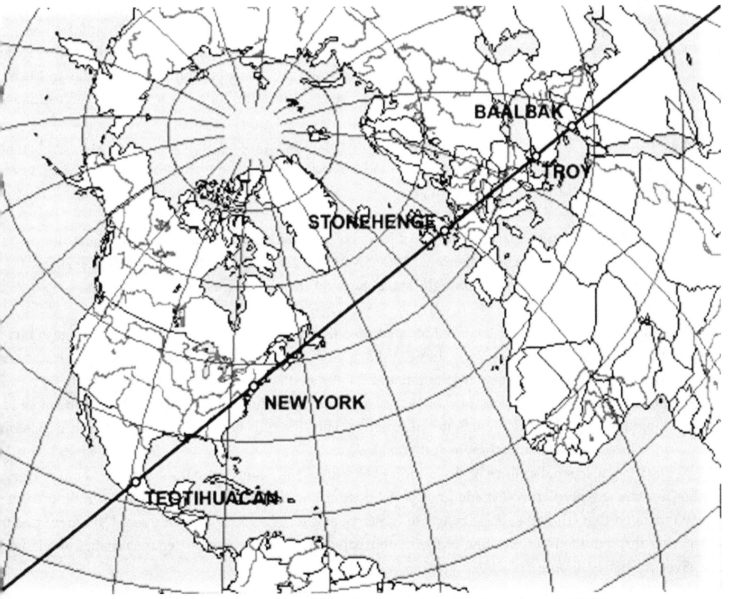

United States primary Ley Line that connects with Stonehenge. *PUB*

and Salem area an entire network was created and established. While the Vortice is considered an Energy Core, the connection lines are called Magick Ley Lines.

Temples in ancient times were intentionally built on Ley Lines to enhance the power of energy and workings of various Paganistic rituals. Ley Lines were also known as Faerie Paths, Corpse Roads, Death Roads or Funerary Paths, Paths of the Wee Folk, and by a number of other names and designations throughout Europe.

The major Ley Line in the Boston area emanates from Stonehenge and travels in a straight line to connect Baalbek in Lebanon; Syria; Temple of the Feathered Serpent in Mexico; New Orleans, Baltimore, New York, Boston and beyond. The Ley Line in Boston specifically passes through the Grand Lodge of Massachusetts and passes through Nahant. A Ley Line may be short or miles long but it will have an estimated width of five and a half feet wide in most cases.

The terminology "Ley-line" was discarded by Mr. Alfred Watkins who, in 1929, began to refer to his calculations and alignments as "old straight tracks" and "archaic tracks." The concept was not accepted, but in various works this terminology remains in place. According to Wikipedia, the definition of "Ley Lines" is

> "...hypothetical alignments of a number of places of geographical interest, such as ancient monuments and megaliths. Their existence was suggested in 1921 by the amateur archaeologist Alfred Watkins, whose book 'The Old Straight Track' brought the alignments (wider) attention..."

According to recent research, the Ley Line that runs through Nahant originates at Stonehenge and circumnavigates the earth. There are two sites that have been listed, between Little and Big Nahant, in the vicinity of the former U.S. Coast Guard Station and Bayley's Hill. Closely following the Ley Line in North America is the *Northeast Megalopolis*, also known as the Boston-Washington Corridor, which is the most urbanized agglomeration in the United States of America. This line runs northeast to southwest from Boston, New York City, Philadelphia, Baltimore and Washington, DC.

There are also smaller lines of distinction in this area. Mr. Jean Gottmann, a learned French Geographer, researched, studied and made known the Boston-Washington Corridor in 1961. Mr. Gottmann's study indicated that while the major cities are "discrete and independent" they are also "uniquely tied to each other through the inter-meshing of their suburban zones, taking on some characteristics of a single massive city: a megalopolis."

Quite often remnants from a gathering or ritual may be found atop Bayley's Hill, while at other times only campfire ashes remain from midnight rituals. There have been Paganistic ceremonies in Nahant, bu ot of a malevolent manner. A number have been orchestrated upon Bayley's Hill, while others have been

n private homes.

The Author extends his sincere appreciation to Madame Llaluna Pellegrina, Right Reverend Arch Priest-

ss of the Temple of Ancient Wisdom, in England, and her associate, Madame Madelein Swart, Priestess

t Capetown, South Africa, for their benevolence in acquainting the author with Wicca and a rudimentary

iew into this most fascinating, meaningful, and ancient religion that remains in peaceful practice and har-

nony today.

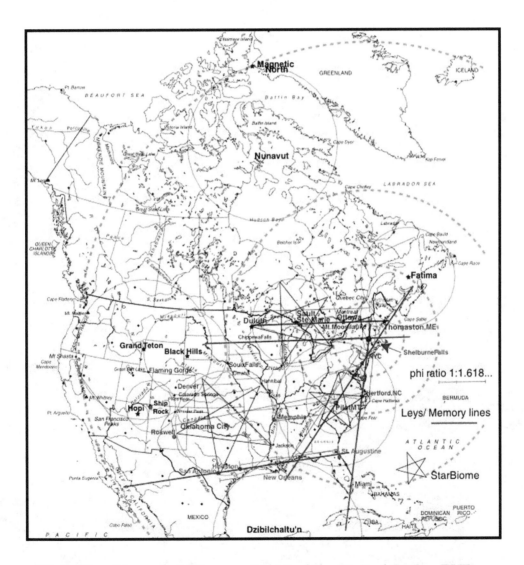

Major Ley Lines and Memory Lines of the United States. *PUB*

Chapter Four

Sea serpent Part I

Enter the Sea serpent... In the early times, the sea off the Massachusetts coast was a dangerous place for sailing vessels and remained so for countless generations. Accordingly, the Commonwealth had its share of high-sea drama, legends, and sailors' salty tales. There were few more entertaining than that of the Sea serpent that cruised Massachusetts Bay. The Native Americans in the area often spoke of a large snake that was seen in coastal waters in the areas which later became known as Lynn and Gloucester.

Sightings of a sea serpent, or sea monster, were first recorded in Massachusetts waters during the early 1600s. Documented in "A Book of New England Legends and Folk Lore" (Samuel Adams Drake, 1884), the initial sighting of the monster was in Gloucester in 1638. Mr. John Josselyn Gent wrote:

> "Coiled up on a rock at Cape Ann by a passing boat, and that when an Englishman would
> have fired at him, an Native hastily prevented his doing so, saying that it would bring them
> ill luck."

His observation would remain and haunt the Massachusetts coastline for centuries thereafter.

The sea serpent was also observed in the vicinity of Nahant, which was then recognized as "Nahantus," lowing swimming past the peninsula and between Egg Rock, then known the as *Bird's Egg Rock*. Soon the sea creature became known as the Gloucester Sea Serpent. At this point it began to be a common visitor to Massachusetts waters. In 1641, in an account by Mr. Obediah Turner, the following incident near Lynn was documented:

An early artist's ink rendering of a sea serpent. From an old print. *UNK*

"Some being on ye great beache gathering of calms and seaweed whch had been cast thereon by ye mightie storm did spy a most wonderful serpent a shorte way off from ye shore. He was big round in ye thickest part as a wine pipe; and they do affirm that he was fifteen fathoms [90 feet] or more in length. A most wonderful tale. But ye witnesses be credible, and it would be of no account to them to tell an untrue tale. Wee have likewise heard yt Cape Ann ye people have seene a monster like unto this, whch did there come out of ye land mch to ye terror of them yt did see him."

Following these reports, little was seen of the sea serpent until a brief sighting off the Maine coast in 1751. Very little of sea monsters was mentioned until 1793. A Captain and crew of a large sailing vessel off Mount Desert Island in Maine waters observed what they thought was a sea serpent resting on the open sea. The captain and crew all stated that the sea creature was longer and larger than their 85 ton sloop. Simultaneously, a large sea serpent was observed near Pemaquid Point and Muscongus Island and months later at Mount Desert Island. During the early 1800s, an aggregate of six individual sightings were documented near Fox and Long Islands in Maine. The early summer season of the 1800s commenced with numerous sightings and observations of a sea serpent. Hundreds of spectators, on shore and in watercraft

Another early artist's ink rendering of the Glouceser Sea serpent, covered in armored scales. *UNK*

spotted the sea creature in 1817 off Cape Ann. Newspapers and gazettes quickly made note of the occurrence, amplifying the stories of a sea monster in Massachusetts Bay. Newspapers and fliers were circulated concerning the "wonderful sea snake" and the countless witnesses who had observed it. On August 12th, 1817, numerous persons observed the sea snake in Gloucester Harbor. On the 14th he was observed, once again, and on the following day he was seen in the waters off Nahant. When the creature was observed, news spread quickly and hundreds of curious spectators ran to the beach to see the creature. Simultaneously, a goodly number of small boats, crowded with curious men and ladies, were launched from Swampscott to see the monster closely. Spectators that were close to the creature estimated that it was between 80 to 90 feet in length.

On August 18th, 1817, in answer to the numerous sightings and public curiosity, the Linnean Society of Boston formed a committee, "for the purpose of collecting any evidence which may exist respecting a remarkable animal, denominated a Sea Serpent, reported to have been seen in and near the Harbour of Gloucester."

Shortly thereafter, Colonel Thomas Handasyd Perkins visited Gloucester Harbor with pointed interest to observe the sea monster. He positioned himself at the edge of Eastern Point to satisfy himself "that the report in circulation was not a fable." Shortly after his arrival he noticed "an agitation moving 5 - 10 miles per

EGG ROCK AND THE SEA-SERPENT.

A detailecd ink rendering of the Nahant Sea serpent, off Bird's Egg Rock. *PUB*

hour." The Colonel commented that, 'I had no doubt that what I had seen was the sea serpent in pursuit o fish."The Sea serpent was sighted at all hours of the day while most of the witnesses stated that it appeared to be an enormous snake, black or dark brown in color with white lower segment and an overall length o seventy to one hundred feet in length, and a diameter of three feet. The head was generally considered to be serpentine in nature, with a long tongue and two bright eyes. Officially, the creature was designated "a strange marine animal."

A small pamphlet was published by a local committee in December, 1817. It contained, in addition to data, the sworn depositions of twelve witnesses. All of the witnesses but one saw an identical sea monster Most of the sightings and observations were seen near the entrance to Gloucester Harbor as it frequented that area from the 10th through the 23rd of August. On August 28th, it was seen headed northward and on 3rd and 5th of October it was seen in Long Island Sound. In the August 1819 issue of <u>The United States Jour nal,</u> a document was published from a most reputable spectator who observed the Sea serpent off Nahant

"I had with me an excellent telescope. When I reached the strand I found many persons as-
sembled, and soon afterward I saw appear at a short distance from the shore, an animal whose

Artist's ink rendering of the Nahant Sea serpent, from an 1833 print. *PUB*

body formed a series of blackish curves, of which I counted thirteen; other persons estimated the number at fifteen. The monster passed thrice at a moderate speed, traversing the bay, whose waters writhed in foam under its huge bulk. We could easily calculate that its length could not be less than fifty or sixty feet. This at least I can affirm, without presuming to say to what species belongs the animal which I have just seen, that, at least, it was neither a whale nor cachalot, nor any strong souffleur, nor any other enormous cetacean. None of those gigantic animals have such an undulating back."

Following that document was another, a deposition to the officials of Essex County, Massachusetts:

"I, the undersigned, Gresham Bennett, second master, declare that on the 6th of June at 7 a.m., while navigating on board the sloop Concord, on her way from New York to Salem, the vessel being about fifteen miles from Race Point, in sight of Cape St. Anne, I heard the helmsman cry out and call me, saying that there was something close to the ship well worth looking at." "I ran immediately to the side he pointed out and saw a serpent of enormous magnitude floating on the water. Its head rose about seven feet above the surface; the weather was clear and the sea calm. The color of the animal in all its visible parts was black, and the skin appeared smooth and free from scales. Its head was about as long as that of a horse, but was the perfect head of a serpent, terminating on the upper part in a flattened surface. We could not distinguish its eyes.

"I saw it clearly from seven to eight minutes; it swam in the same direction as the sloop and nearly as quickly. Its back consisted of humps or rings the size of a large barrel, separated by intervals of about three feet. These rings appeared fixed and resembled a chain of hogsheads fastened together; the tail was beneath the water. The part of the animal which I actually saw measured about fifteen feet in length; the movement of its rings seemed undulatory."

In the following year Boston merchants surmised that if there was, indeed, a sea monster, it would mea worldwide recognition resulting in untold wealth and prestige. Fortunes were invested by Gloucester an nearby townships in fitting out boats and crews to hunt the sea serpent. Boats of all sizes were fitted wit harpoons and trained whaling harpoonmen, in hopes of finding and capturing the elusive sea monster.

On August 13th and 14th, 1819, the sea serpent was observed off Nahant where it remained in the sur rounding waters for some weeks. It was also seen in Boston's outer harbor, but it never ventured into th

A common, though somewhat morbid, view of a sea serpent with its victim. *PUB*

ort itself. Over two hundred persons observed the creature, all giving identical descriptions. The creature maintained thirteen humps, or folds, on its back, while its serpentine head was erect at least two feet above he water. Another noteworthy personage, Mr. Benjamin F. Newhall of Saugus, witnessed the sea serpent ff Nahant. "As he turned short," Newhall described, "the snakelike form became apparent, bending like n eel. I could plainly see what appeared to be from 50 to 70 feet in length. Behind his head appeared a uccession of bundles or humps upon his back."

At the same time, the sea serpent was observed off Nahant by a goodly number of shoreline specta-ors including Messrs. Samuel Cabot, James Magee, and Thomas Handasyd Perkins. The sea monster had ecome extremely popular and seeing it became a quest for visitors to the great Nahant Hotel. Due to the nterest, the hotel requested a well known composer to create a polka for the sea serpent. The polka quickly ecame popular and was played quite frequently. However, sightings of the sea serpent became infrequent n successive years.

In 1826, it appeared off Nahant, in an incident recorded by the <u>Lynn Mirror</u> newspaper. Little was doc-umented of the sighting, as it was a goodly distance off the shore, and general interest had begun to wane. even years later, in July, 1833, the Sea serpent appeared off Nahant, once again.

"It was first seen on Saturday afternoon," the <u>Lynn Mirror</u> described, "passing between Egg Rock and he Promontory, winding into Lynn Harbour; and again on Sunday morning, heading for South Shores. It vas seen by forty or fifty ladies and gentlemen, who insist that they could not have been deceived."

The most noted incident in the hunt for the sea serpent concerned Captain Richard Rich of Boston, who ommanded a well-equipped vessel and a well manned crew to search for the behemoth. The craft was well quipped for any circumstance and, with much fanfare from onlookers, sailed from Boston into Massachu-etts Bay. The shorelines were carefully scrutinized for three days without seeing any form of sea serpent. According to the <u>Boston Daily Advertiser</u> in 1819, Captain Rich and crew formulated a report that they had, most assuredly, found the sea monster, "or what had been taken for one..."

A multitude of curiosity-seekers went to see the Sea serpent, only to be greatly disappointed to find that t was a "horse macquerel," or, an uncommonly large example of a common pelagic fish. Indignation flared n the Boston newspapers and the story was carried along the eastern seaboard from Maine all the way to New Orleans. Captain Rich's "hoax" eventually turned against him with future sightings of a serpent, and is "sea serpent" mackerel became known as "Rich's Folly." Immediately following his revelation, though, eports of the sea serpent terminated and those who did see one dared not report it due to public ridicule.

Nevertheless sightings persisted, although quietly.

Chapter Five

Sea serpent Part II

Enter the Nahant sea serpent... Whether by faith or through observation, there were those who never believed in the "giant mackerel" theory about the sea serpent. Documented reports of the serpent began once again in 1838 when the following lighthearted article about the supposedly harmless creature appeared in the <u>Daily Herald,</u> Newburyport, Massachusetts, issue 302, Volume V, dated Saturday, July 20, 1839:

"The Sea Serpent has just commenced his annual cruise off Nahant. His 'estimated' length is about the same as usual, and he is said to be in good condition and quite playful."

Other articles from various newspapers and publications kept the reader of 1839 well informed of the appearances and locations of the sea serpent. One such article appears on the following page and concerns a sighting by Captain Sturgis and crew of the United States Revenue Cutter *Hamilton*.

In years to follow, it became quite a sport for visitors at the coast to glimpse and watch the sea serpent off Nahant or along the Lynn shoreline. Following the conflagration of the Nahant Hotel at East Point, sightings began to wane, in turn followed by disinterest in the sea creature.

Perhaps one of the most recognized and documented sightings of a sea serpent took place not off Bird's Egg Rock or Gloucester, but by the Royal Naval Corvette *H.M.S. Daedalus*. The incident took place on the sixth of August, 1848, when a mainmast lookout alerted the captain and crew of a sea creature of enormous size. Captain Peter M'Quhae, also listed as M'Quile, his officers and members of the crew, all observed the massive creature as it turned in a slow circle and directed itself toward the war craft. Captain Peter M. Quhae's official report stated:

The Daily Herald.

PUBLISHED EVERY MORNING, BY JOSEPH B MORSS & WM. H. BREWSTER, AT NO. 11, CORNHILL.

VOL. VII.   NEWBURYPORT, SATURDAY, JULY 20, 1839.   NO. 302.

THE DAILY HERALD $5,00
SEMI-WEEKLY HERALD $4,00
TERMS OF ADVERTISING. Advertisements not exceeding six lines are inserted for 75 cents,—seven lines and upwards, $1,—per square, $1.25—more than a square, at the same rate. Probate Notices agreeably to the customary prices.
The privilege of annual advertisers is lim-

GUARDIAN'S SALE.
VALUABLE REAL ESTATE.
To be sold at Public Auction, on THURS-DAY, the 1st day of August, at 10 o'clock, at the mansion house of the late Nathanie Knapp, in Middle street—
A two story Dwelling House on Middle street, convenient for two families, with about 20 rods

THE WIVES OF THE DEAD.
BY N. HAWTHORNE.
The following story, the simple and do-mestic incidents of which may be deemed scarcel worth relating, after a lapse of time, awakened some degree of interest a hundred years ago, in a principal seaport of the Bay Province. The rainy twilight of an autumn

in love a power that love had won. The cheering radiance of the fire had shone upon the happy circle, and the dead glimmer of the lamp might have befitted their reunion now. While Margaret groaned in bitterness, she heard a knock at the street door.
'How would my heart have leaped at that sound but yesterday!' thought she, remem-bering the

THE SEA SERPENT. Capt. Sturgis of the Revenue Cutter Hamilton, arrived at this port yesterday from Cape Ann, having been cruising two or three days in the bay. He informs us that on Wednesday afternoon, when off Nahant, he and all his officers and crew had a fair view of the Sea Serpent. The appearance of this marine monster was such as has been often before described. The sea was at the time perfectly smooth, and the Sea Serpent was only about twice the length of the vessel distant from them, after remaining in sight a few minutes, he sunk down into the water and disappeared. [Boston Gazette.

Newspaper headliner and article from a period newspaper concerning the great sea serpent off Nahant as witnessed from the United States Revenue Cutter *Hamilton*. The article is dated July 20, 1839. Newspaper: <u>The Daily Herald</u>, Newburyport, Massachusetts. Volume VII, Issue Number 302

"It was discovered to be an enormous serpent, with head and shoulders kept about four feet constantly above the surface of the sea; and as nearly as we could approximate by comparing it with the length of what our maintopsail-yard would show in the water, there was at the very least sixty feet of the animal a *fleur d'eau* no portion of which was, to our perception, used in propelling it through the water, either by vertical or horizontal undulation. It passed rapidly, but so close under our lee quarter that had it been a man of my acquaintance I should have easily recognized the features with the naked eye."

The *HMS Daedalus*, from the October 1848 issue of the Illustrated London News, headlining. *RNA*

Detail of the Sea serpent viewed from the *HMS Daedalus*. October, 1848 article *RNA*

The report was carried in many countries, but its main interest was in New England waters. Despite the positive description by the Royal Navy, the sea serpent's recorded activity in New England's waters began to diminish.

Although there were sightings during the summer in following years, it appeared as if the sea creature was hibernating or had gone to another area. Activity began during the 1870s when a witness described his--or her--sighting to a local newspaper in Plymouth, Massachusetts. On July 17, 1875, a sea serpent was observed near Plymouth in Cape Cod Bay. Captain Garton of the vessel *S.S. Norman* saw the

Coiled surface seaweed was initially thought to be a sea serpent. *PUB*

creature on the surface of the water. His statement was verified by both passengers and crew of the *S.S. Roman*, nearby.

A few days later, on July 30, 1875, Messrs. Arthur Lawrence, F.W. Lawrence, and other people of quality, were aboard the yacht *Princess* between Egg Rock and Nahant. A Sea serpent was observed and followed for two hours. The creature had a black upper surface and a white underside with a head resembling a snake or turtle. It appeared similar to a seal, with a small fin or perhaps two situated on the back of its neck. The neck was estimated as having a diameter of 2.5 feet.

Two local fishermen, Mr. Jack Kelsoe and Mr. J.P. Thomas, both from Swampscott, were also in the vicinity as the *Princess* chased the sea serpent, and later testified to the sightings and activities. Two years thereafter, a goodly number of fishermen, boaters, tourists, and bystanders along the shorelines of Nahant, Swampscott, and Gloucester, saw another sea monster. _The Boston Globe_, dated July 19th, 1877, reported,

"That shiny sea serpent which has been such a terror along the New England coast during the past few years has made his debut in Nahant waters this season. He was seen on Monday and again this morning, and the circumstances of his presence are given in such detail by astonished beholders that there is general credence given to the statement that an unusual and prodigious serpentine monster is [displaying] himself in the waters of Massachusetts Bay.

"The first discovery was made by a pleasure party on King's Beach, at about 4 o'clock Monday afternoon, who say that all of them, nine in number, observed about half a mile from shore between themselves and Egg Rock, moving with great rapidity, what could have been nothing else than a huge fish or snake. They say it was perfectly calm at the time, and a large part of the body's length was visible above the water line, as was observed in Gloucester during the 1800s.

"The observers had glasses which enabled them to see distinctly that the strange monster was of an unusual species, and there are many around here who believe it to be a veritable sea serpent. There is of course considerable excitement all along the beach, and some old fishermen who were out early this morning have added to the general commotion by claiming that they too got a momentary

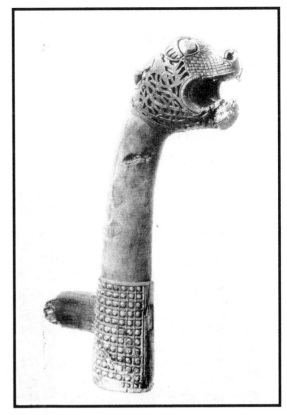

A Viking war craft bow piece evocative of a sea serpent. *GWB*

glimpse of the mysterious stranger. This latter report would not be regarded of much account but for the fact that when the fishermen told their story they had not heard of the discovery made by other parties on Monday. They say they only saw it for a moment, that it seemed to be about 30 feet in length, and was meandering through the water with head slightly elevated, and at times nearly the whole body would seem to rise partially up out of the water.

"The summer visitors here are not skeptical about the monster being of a snaky species, and the citizens are, many of them, of the opinion that he is nothing short of a veritable sea serpent. The same or a similar one was reported along the coast several times last summer, and on one occasion his identity was vouched for in enthusiastic earnest by the officers, crew and entire lot of passengers on board one of the Philadelphia steamers, who sighted the strange being a few miles below Boston Light."

Some enterprising New England newspaper reporters alleged that the sea serpent was "a seasonal sea serpent," and only appeared to the whim of summer visitors. One reporter wrote that harking back to the time of the Norsemen, "it may be also noted that the sea serpent's head was nearly identical to that of a Viking warship's bow sprite." Despite the negative publicity, it remained quite popular and visitors hoped to view it while staying at local hotels along the shore.

During June, 1884, Reverend John George Wood began a research project that required much research and studied all observation and findings of sea serpents in Massachusetts Bay.

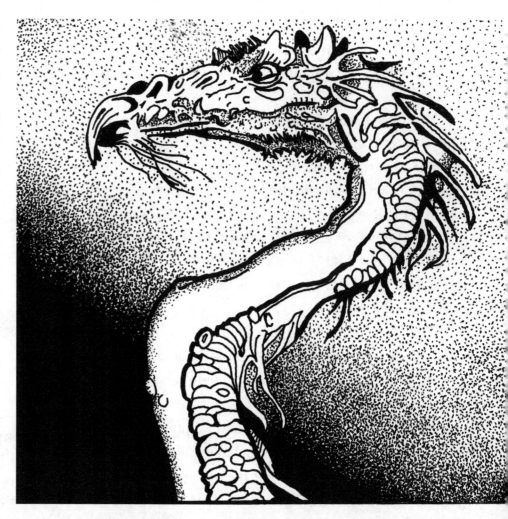

Variation of an old print of a sea serpent. *GWB*

The earliest witness to a sea serpent focused on an incident that took place in 1823.

An elderly but reliable witness, Mr. Francis Johnson of Swampscott, gave his recollection of an incident that took place on the twelfth of July, 1823. Mr. Johnson meticulously related the incident that he had observed of an object in the water heading into Swampscott harbor from the vicinity of Nahant and Egg Rock. Being in constant view of the object, he realized after two hours, that the object was a large sea serpent.

In addition to Mr. Johnson's statement and observations, Reverend Wood amassed a number of sighting for his document and, when possible, spoke with reliable witness. The sea serpent was not seen again for a number of weeks when it was later observed and followed but, unfortunately, no further documentation was filed.

In his research, Reverend Wood also created lengthy chapters that spoke of numerous sea serpent variations. Additionally, the work contained superb illustrations and highly detailed line drawings.

His work contends that,

> "The affidavits of a great many individuals of unblemished character are collected, which leaves no room to apprehend anything like deceit. They do not agree in every minute particular, but in regard to its great length and snake-like form, they are harmonious."

Sightings and first person accounts appeared on the front pages of New England newspapers for many years. A tally of sightings was published, including twelve sightings in 1839, nine in 1875, and nine more in 1886.

Cecil The Sea Sick Sea Serpent, fanciful creation of the author. *GWB*

This represents a total documentation of 190 sightings in one-hundred years! Sightings have diminished during the 20th century with only an aggregate of 56 sea serpent sightings recorded, and all of those were before 1950. A goodly number of naturalists and marine scientists have indicated that the sea serpent was incorrectly identified by excited observers. Their explanations varied from the serpent being a string of dolphins, an elephant seal, or a mass of debris floating with the current on the surface. The only proof of a sea serpent or serpents are statements, verbal documentation, and artists' renderings. A sea serpent has never been photographed, while some of the more fanciful descriptions and sightings were categorized as hoaxes and fantasy.

The explanation of the disappearance of the New England sea serpent is theorized by author J.P. O'Neill in his book <u>The Great New England Sea Serpent</u>. Mr. O'Neill states that the deterioration of the formerly fertile fishing grounds of Massachusetts Bay and along the New England coastline by over-fishing have forced the creature, or creatures, to seek fertile feeding grounds elsewhere, or that they have become extinct.

Notably, the creature or creatures were never given widely accepted names. It, or they, existed and remain in memory merely as "the sea serpent."

Chapter Six

The Devill's Footprints

Enter the devill... There are two separate accounts of the Devill's Footprints at East Point, Nahant. Both instances were in the vicinity of the northwestern side of the point, facing Bird's Egg Rock. The first instance took place on August 1st, 1637, when a visitor observed indentations in the solid rock at East Point, Nahant:

"Some declare ye have seene at Nahantus, sundry wonderful tracks in ye solid rocke, as of some beaste like unto a greate oxe."

Few had interest in the prints, until July 14th, 1650, when the following incident took place. The circumstance was recorded by Mr. Obadiah Turner:

"1650. Iulie, ye 14: Some youngsters being in ye woodes on ye last Lord his day did wickedlie play at cardes on a flat rock. And while ye game was going on, they say there did appeare vpon ye solid rock, in ye middest of them, a foote printe, plaine as a foote printe could be made vpon ye sand of ye beache; whereupon they were greatlie terrified, as well they might be. Ye goode people say yt jt be ye devill his foote printe. But it seemeth strange yt ye devill should desire to drive them off from doing hjs own worke or to disturbe ye breakers of ye Lord hjs daie, or other euil doers. But by whomsoever ye miracle was wrought, methinks it was meant as a solemn warning to Sabbath breakers and card players. And my praier to God is yt jt may be rightlie heeded."

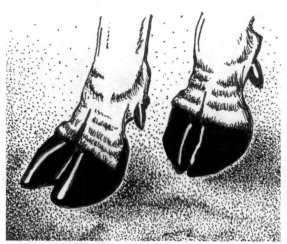

The Devill's cloven feet. *GWB*

Immediately following the boy's proclamation of not follow-ing the Sabbath Day rules, and pleading forgiveness, a number of clergy and religious persons quickly journeyed to Nahant to see and verify the cloven impression. The area in question was a large flat rock which jutted out near the high tide line. The rock in question may still retain faint imprints, but it is highly doubt-ful. There has been much erosion in that area since 1650, and the rock may be either under water or scoured clean by wave action of storms and time itself.

The foot print was clearly viewed, and as found shortly there-after, much to the amazement of the viewers, there were twenty such foot prints, all four inches wide with identical size and of a cloven configuration, all in a straight line, twelve inches apart and all in solid stone. This caused great con-cern and fear from nearby inhabitants in Lynn and Swampscott. The site quickly became considered evil. A number of thoughts were committed to the record by religious and noteworthy men, with general consen-sus that it was the work of "the evil one to plague the settlers." Little more was recorded and the incident was largely forgotten as time passed.

The next recorded incident took place on the eighth of February, 1855, in East and South Devon, En-gland. Following a long night of snowfall, a 60 to 100 mile long string of mysterious footprints were discov-ered. Cloven in nature, and appearing to be scorched into the snow, the footprints went in a straight line over houses, through locked gates, up and over trees, and across areas impossible to access. The distance of the footprints was unnerving, and no answer has yet to be found. According to newspapers it was the Devill playing impish pranks on various townships.

A similar occurrence took place near the same area on March 9, 2009, but only for 60 to 70 feet in length. The last incident of the Devill's footprints on Nahant occurred in the early 1860s, shortly after the confla-gration that consumed the Great Nahant Hotel.

Enter Mr. Abel Ballard, a man local to Nahant and talented in many ways, being a blacksmith, fisher-man, sportsman, and drunkard, who was further described as lazy, ignorant, and very much reckless. He decided to row to Egg Rock for a private feast. He took a keg of rum, fishing line, his revolver, and other things necessary for "a right jolly time." Within a very short period, Abel caught a number of fish and in

The Great Nahant Hotel ruins seen from the Mifflin Estate.Image by John Amory Codman

the rocky recess near the top of Egg Rock, near the lighthouse, he found a number of bird's eggs. He built a fire and cooked the fish and eggs complete with condiments he brought and created a sumptuous meal for himself. Abel saw the lighthouse keeper, but only a friendly wave was exchanged between them.

Following his feast, he took a rest, sleeping for a few hours. When he woke, he discovered that it was quickly growing dark. He also noticed a very fast-moving, threatening, dark cloud approaching and the sound of thunder beyond Boston. He quickly put all of his belongings into his boat and began rowing toward Lynn. He reached for his "dear companion," only to find the keg was left on Egg Rock. He hastily put about, returned to Egg Rock, retrieved his keg and furiously began to row toward the mainland. At that point he realized he was not going to reach Lynn in time but East Point was closer and more favorable.

With the aid of an opportune wave, he finally reached East Point in a cove that was later recognized as

"Lodge Beach," or, as Northeastern Marine Science now has it labeled, "Dive Beach." Abel secured the boat in the small cove. In the distance the debris of the old Nahant Hotel stood and through a small wooded area a small shed was seen. He threw himself on the floor of the shed and passed out from fatigue and spirits.

The storm struck with fury and about midnight Abel was awakened by a tremendous clap of thunder, bolts of lightning and sheets of rain. Continuous lightning illuminated a "strange hairy object of about the size of a stout man" that entered the door of the shed. The monster, erect in nature, uttered a long, broad laugh and when it

Representation of the Devill playing at the East Point, Nahant cliffs. *GWB*

opened its mouth from its dog-like head, it extended its long, red tongue in a most horrendous manner. It began to move as if it was playing a fiddle and dance in a "fantastic style." Abel, still lying on the floor, remained speechless. The thing stopped, told Abel he was dancing for him and in a unearthly voice asked if he would dance with him. Abel did not rise and the form commanded him to do so, again informing him that it would be good to have a "merry round." Abel was much too frightened and didn't trust his limbs to function. Called a "jolly old toper," Abel remained prostrate until the form stated "he was as dry as a fish" and required drink. He added if Abel did not divulge the location of his keg, "he would give him a kick that would send him back to Egg Rock, and thence, by a bounce, to the Swampscott shore."

He raised his foot and at that instance, Abel realized the form had a large cloven foot. The form grasped Abel, who said that his keg was in the boat. The form laughed long and loudly and departed the shed, leaving the pungent aroma of brimstone. From exhaustion, Abel passed out once more.

East Point and the meadow area that Mr. Abel Ballard landed during the storm. Winter, 2019. *ABG*

A bright sun awoke Abel. He tried to put his mind in order as it labored and roiled. He left the shed and as he looked down into the cove, found his damaged boat placed high on rocks while all the boat's cargo was missing. With hair on end and stiffened jaw he stood sightlessly gazing toward Egg Rock. Then he looked down to see imprinted in the solid rock, impressions of cloven feet. Able had no doubt now that his midnight visitor was none other but the Devill, as no human could leave such footprints. This realization fueled Abel with considerable powers of locomotion. In utter frustration, he yelled and began running and did not stop until he had run more than a mile, losing his hat and one shoe. He met a teamster going down to the shore for seaweed. But the man was quite leery to give him assistance, as he acted so wild and appeared to be in such a questionable state of mind. Abel was eventually recognized, and related what occurred. The teamster listened to Abel's account, who seemed to have unquestionably seen a devil, but

Aerial image of the seaward facing cliff and beach area of East Point, c. 2018. *DAV*

the teamster questioned if it was a devil of his mind and nowhere else. The man was quick to inform Abe that "more devils come from rum kegs than from brimstone beds," and expressed a hope that as the one in question had now sailed away with the old keg he would not get a new keg to breed any more.

Abel was convinced that the evil one had paid him a visit. He brought many doubters to those hideou footprints, and pointed to the rock where his boat was placed as proof. If the impressions were ever there they were probably made at the earliest period in the earth's history when other mysterious impression existed. However, if they did exist, it is not imaginable that they yet remain or will come to light again.

Assuming that the footprints were there, Abel may indeed have been the first white man who saw them though surely others had seen them prior. The waves, no doubt, battered his boat and lodged it upon the rock where he found it. Finally, the teamster was no doubt right in his opinion of the evil spirit, quoted fo posterity as saying "Delirium tremens often furnishes those optics keen that enable people to see what i not to be seen."

Hard proof of this encounter may never be found. Shortly after this incident, the Lodge family construct

East Point's last major military construction project, the Army's Nike-Ajax Missile System, c. 1955. *USA*

d a beautiful mansion near this location. In years to follow, the United States Army Engineers constructed a massive gun battery atop the area in question. Blasting and leveling of the ground during construction may well have eradicated all proof of the Devill's footprints.

During the Cold War, East Point was chosen to be a U. S. Army Nike-Ajax Missile Station. The system was divided into segments: the launcher area was to be at East Point, while the control site was at Bayley's Hill. Many tons of fill and rock were brought to East Point on a daily basis. Blasting was commonplace. Except at the tide level, much of East Point has been dramatically altered since Abel's harrowing day.

But then, perhaps the Devill's footprints still remain, whether beneath the weight of earthen fill or removed during construction and relocated to parts unknown.

Chapter Seven

Neptune's Temple

Enter the Grand Park of Nahant... In 1859, a Grand Park was created in Nahant. It was established along the present Marginal Road, being split by Ocean Street. Created by the Honorable Frederick Tudor, also known as the "Ice King," who created and began the ice trade in this country. He designed and had constructed delightful gardens, walkways, pavilions, and a small amusement park within.

The park was bound, by present day locations, Ocean Street, fronted by the ocean, or Marginal Road. The area of interest, "Neptune's Temple," was in Range VIII as established on *"Plan of Ranges, 7, 8 & 9 Nahant,* by F. Tudor and R. Tappan.

When complete, Mr. Tudor called it "Maolis," from "Siloam" transposed. Siloam was an ancient site in Jerusalem and remains one of the few undisputed locations within its metes and bounds. The park and garden became quite popular and boasted walkways, small amusements for children, and rides for adults. Later, a refreshment stand was added and a small admission fee was requested to enter and enjoy the park.

One of the features in the park, that remains in place today, was "Neptune's Temple." Considered a retreat, it was an octagonal, gabled wood and stone structure placed between and shaded by balm-of-Gilead trees. The structure had an eight gabled roof that was supported by eight pillars of unfinished stone, carefully selected for texture and color, positioned and cemented together.

Both roof and gables were covered with sturdy hemlock bark, while each gable had round gilded wooden medallions of various mythological sea creatures fixed to it. On top of the structure was a large weather vane made of wood that consisted of a sea shell with gilded scalloped edges borne aloft by two satyrs that would radiate in the sunshine. When completed, the imposing structure maintained an overall diameter of 125 feet, with a ceiling height of twelve to fifteen feet, depending on the angle of the base. The designer was John Q. Hammond, selected by Frederick Tudor personally, who also supervised the structure's construction. Assisting him was his fourteen year old son who designed and fashioned the decorations and medallions.

The solid platform gave a spectacular view of Lynn, Swampscott, and Marblehead, together with Bird's Egg Rock, with its lighthouse and, of course, the open sea. Underlying the pavilion was a small natural cave that was enlarged into a den that Tudor called the "Cave of the Lion." Simultaneously, knowledge that an accused witch had been sheltered in the small cave in 1692 was emphasized.

Tudor wanted something unique for his cave. He contracted Mr. David Hunt, a local mason, to sculpt a ferocious lion of stone for the inside of the cave. Mr. Hunt completed the ferocious stone lion and when it was placed in the entry to the den, Mr. Tudor was so pleased, he contracted for another to be placed near the front entrance to Maolis. A sturdy set of iron bars were fashioned into the stone foundation of the temple, keeping the silent lion caged. During this time the name of the site changed to "Maolis Gardens." The original name of the imposing structure was "Neptune's Temple," which soon changed to become the "Rock Temple."

The cage or den containing the stone lion became known as the "Cave of the Lion," and at varying periods, the temple itself was recognized as such. Later still, the structure was recognized as the "Witch Temple," and the cave below became known as "The Lion's Den." At the beginning of the last century it was simply called the "Witch House," an appellation which remains in place through the present time.

Although Maolis Gardens was dismantled in 1892, the pavilion remains en situ. The medallions and weather vane have long disappeared, except one, the sea serpent, which surfaced recently and sold for $7,000. All of the medallions were of exquisitely carved and gilded wood, approximately thirty-one inches in diameter, and had been mounted on the peak of each gable. The sea serpent figural medallion consisted of a winged serpent with a swirled tail carved in relief and mounted upon a round, black painted wooden plaque.

The rear was engraved with the name "R.C. Wilson." In 1985, the medallion was purchased from the estate of Royal C. Nelson, a resident of Nahant, whose name was also impressed on the medallion's back.

The Witch's Den

The "Witch House" also has a most interesting history. During the *"Great Outbreak of 1692,"* when the dark side of witchcraft appeared in nearby Salem, those suspected of witchcraft were hunted and brought

"Neptune's Temple" depicting medallions and "The Lion Den" below, c. 1870. *PUB*

o trial. The victims, mostly innocent of all accusations, may well have been people with unfortunate mala-
dies not recognized in that era. It was a black period in the chapters of New England's history. If a person
was suspected of witchcraft he or she would be summoned and brought by the sheriff to court, placed in
front of a magistrate, and their fate would be decided.

Nineteen women were convicted of witchcraft from June through September 1692, in the greater Lynn
and Salem area. They were brought, by cart, to Proctor's Ledge, formerly thought to be Gallow's Hill in
Salem, and hung until dead. One 80 year old man was "pressed" *(Peine Forte Et Dure)* to death, for refusing
to speak. Countless souls were accused of witchcraft, many spending long weeks and months awaiting
trials. Witnesses would be summoned and the accused would be allowed to explain or defend their actions.

Artist's rendition of Mr. David Hunt's lion for the "Cave of the Lion." *GWB*

Many accused were set free after the magistrate concluded there was no just cause for the accusation; others were imprisoned for a short period of time. However, if their defense was questionable, the unfortunate were considered guilty of witchcraft and were punished accordingly.

The four major measures of punishment consisted of hanging, being crushed by beams and weights across their chests, roasted by fire, or dousing, which meant being drowned by constant immersion. In North America, dousing was by means of a "Dunking Stool."

During this dark period of "witch hunts" and superstition, thirteen women and five men had been hung, and one "pressed." In aggregate, more than a hundred people were accused and imprisoned. Several of these souls were from nearby Lynn, Massachusetts.

Enter Miss Sarah Hood... Born in August 1657 in Lynn, Massachusetts, Miss Sarah Hood was the daughter of Mr. Richard Hood, who was married to the former Miss Mary Newhall.

On October 25th, 1675, at eighteen years of age, Sarah married Mr. William Bassett, Junior. In late April 1692, she was accused of witchcraft, but before the sheriff brought her before the magistrate, she escaped with her twenty-two month old child and fled to sanctuary in Nahant.

Her husband brought her to a very small and largely unknown cave and gave her provisions to survive for a short time. The cave was off present day Marginal Road near the corner of Ocean Street.

Conditions in the cave were less than spartan. In addition to a meager food and water supply, the young woman had to be vigilant for wild animals. Sarah's food and water supply quickly dwindled and she was forced to occasionally leave the small cave to forage. Sarah's prime concern was her child. She sacrificed her share of food to keep the child as well as possible. Randomly, as not to cause suspicion, her husband, William Bassett, Junior, brought food, water, and

Neptune's Temple's "sea serpent" medallion. *PUB*

blankets to keep her and the child warm in the small cave. She was eventually discovered by a fisherman as she searched along the water's edge for edibles. Unfortunately for Mrs. Bassett, the outspoken fisherman notified Lynn authorities which resulted in her being captured. She was brought to and tried at Salem on the 23rd of May, 1692. The accusers made their statements, and the magistrate concluded that she would be incarcerated at a prison in Boston for a given time.

Upon entry to prison, Sarah was fitted with a heavy iron shackle secured to her ankle. A sturdy chain attached her child to her. Her jailers spoke little and depression and hopelessness were heavy in the cells. Her female cell companions observed her and remarked she had an "introduction to Irons upon Limbs." Many women had shackles attached to both arms and legs, but Sara had a child and her arms were left free.

Sanitary conditions were nonexistent and the meals arrived in a bucket and a small metal bowl served as an all encompassing utensil. Privacy and cleanliness did not exist. After the long, wretched ordeal of filth, disease, vermin, and unfathomable conditions of prison, she was released on December third, 1692, having served a total of seven months. She and her child went back to her home and husband who resided on Nahant Street in nearby Lynn. Following release, she was awarded nine pounds sterling for compensation for being in prison and being falsely accused of witchcraft. Later, she gave birth to a daughter whom she named "Deliverance," to accent her survival of persecution and her subsequent release from prison. Unfortunately, Miss Deliverance Bassett became known as the "Child of the Witch."

Mrs. Sarah Bassett passed in 1721 at sixty-four years of age. Throughout narrations, the name Bassett has also been incorrectly spelled with but one "t" while Sarah has also been incorrectly listed as Sara.

Above: Mrs. Bassett's cave or later, "The Lion's Den," showing entrance portal and interior. *SEC*
Opposite, top: Miss Sarah Hood, c. 1676. *GWB*
Opposite, left: Departing the "Lion's Den," c. 2019. *SEC*
Opposite, right: Recognized as "The Ledge," or "Proctor's Ledge," this spot is where accused witches' bodies were inserted between rocks and left to be consumed by wildlife or removed by families under cover of darkness and buried in family plots. *UNK*

Chapter Eight

Swallow Cave

Enter the Sea Cave... Swallow Cave is considered a long, deep-channel, natural opening that passes through the land into the sea on two sides. During low tide the cave is completely open and individuals may pass through it at their desire. Access to the interior of the cave is made by a descent down the cliffs on the seaward side while it is a climb down, via steps, to gain access to the entrance. Swallow Cave measures seventy two feet in length, ten feet in width and eight feet in height. Partway through, there remains a slight bend in the passageway.

The walls of the dreary cave remain as being rough and irregular while the uneven floor with its cavities are covered in barnacles. Except during storms, the cave is in perpetual humidity. In times of quiet as when the sea is calm, the sound of water percolating through the fissures in the ceiling and dropping onto the floor remains unending. During storms or on exceptionally windy days, the wind roaring through the cave creates screeching and supernatural howling sounds.

The name Swallow Cave originated when the entire cave was a nesting area and habitat for swallows. The birds built their nests in the upper area upon jutting rocks and ledges. The birds remained in the cave for a goodly portion of the year and some remained during the winter months "in a completely torpid state." Due to the numerous visitors in the late 1800s and early 1900s, the birds relocated elsewhere. Only the name remains.

Also accessible at low tide near the cave is Pea Island, which has been described as a large rock outcrop covered with a little soil, grass, and beach pea (Lathyrus maritimus).

The Legend of Swallow Cave

The legend of Swallow Cave commenced in 1675, during King Phillips War. A Native American raiding party from the south shore of Boston secretly landed near Lynn at the area known as the Saugus River and hid their canoes. The natives quietly made their way through woods and upon arriving at Lynn, attacked the settlement under cover of darkness. The men of Lynn fought back fiercely and pushed the native force back and then toward the ocean and Nahant.

A variation on an ancient rendering of Swallow Cave. *GWB*

The natives quickly escaped over what is now known as the Nahant Causeway and reached the end of the peninsula. The settlers pursued only to the end of the long sandy beach and knew their prey was trapped. A good force of armed settlers were posted at this point in the event the natives tried to escape to their canoes. A large fire consisting of driftwood was lit and the settlers took positions to thwart any attempts of escape. The remainder of the settlers returned to Lynn proper to rest and be with their families, determined to apprehend or annihilate the invaders the following day. Upon return, the Captain of Lynn Militia called his militiamen into action. They marched to the settlers' fire and took positions. The natives may have sent a scout to investigate the situation, but the remainder went to the end of East Point.

When dawn arrived, and the tide was at its lowest ebb, the natives formed into two-man scout teams to explore the island they were held captive. Two of the raiding party's scouts observed that the settlers had established a guard post and camp fire. Additional settlers and militiamen arrived to form a small army, with intent to hunt and annihilate the natives. A small oared boat was launched from Lynn and wa harged with patrolling and observing the sea areas and cliffs of Nahant. The boat carried both rowmen and musketmen at the ready if the natives were observed.

Two of the exploring natives discovered a cave that would be safe refuge during the daylight hours. At a later time, the cave became known as Swallow Cave. While the native warriors were in the cave, they attempted to contact and communicate with the spirit worlds. During this time they practiced traditional native healing techniques along with methods for receiving powers from animals and animal spirits.

A number of days passed and the raiding party was not located. In addition to regular boat patrols the Lynn force also had a heavily armed land patrol. The Captain of Militia quickly trained able settlers in the relevant aspects of warfare and tactics by which the native party would be located and terminated.

The natives seemingly disappeared. In frustration, one of the leading members of the Lynn Militia sought a visionary who resided in nearby Salem Village.

*Enter Witch Wonderful...*During this era, a visionary was someone considered articulate in the art of black magic, but the witch interviewed was considered a "white witch," not desirous of casting dire spells. Visionaries and the like were regarded as folklorist, or, capable of divination prediction. "Witch Wonderful," who resided near the shoreline in Salem, was a brilliant-minded, sharp-tongued woman, and made her living by telling the future and locating lost items and materials.

The afternoon skies were dark. The air was heavy. The Captain of Militia and his lieutenants were invited into her hut and held audience with the woman. Witch Wonderful held a small candle, which accented her wrinkled skin and bright eyes. She evaluated the captain after a period of silence, and stated, "Welcome, my brave soldiers. Success to your enterprise. You see, I know where your game is!"

At that moment her candle blew out and the party was enveloped in complete darkness. The legend continues as Mr. Edward Rowe Snow relates in his 1949 book, *Strange Tales from Nova Scotia to Cape Hatteras*. "Before tomorrow's sun has set," he reports Witch Wonderful saying, "you'll be sure of the wild, yelling devils." Simultaneously, a freshening breeze banged a door shut in a small shed next to her hut.

"Comrades, are we betrayed?" shouted the Captain. "Take care what you say, Wonderful."

"Why, my brisk man," answered Wonderful, "I haven't lived seventy years for a blustery soldier of thirty to question me. I know that you are after the natives, and I know that you will find them, forty in number, on the Nahant shore, waiting to dip their tomahawks into the blood of your families. I've been counting the clouds and watching cattle all week."

Mimicking a child's high voice, she then recited a most curious incantation:

Mingle mingle, mingle mingle,
    Away, apart, together, single,
The Indians on shore you'll see,
    Your death or life - remember me.

The settlers paid homage to Witch Wonderful and in the early morning marched in force to Nahant, as the tide allowed, and formed in the area above Swallow Cave. The settlers and militia surrounded the Natives, with two small oared boats near the cave's entrance and exit. Each of the twenty-five settlers and militia men were armed

Natives departing peacefully. *GWB*

with broadsword and musket, some both, while all carried "a Bible in his hand and a Westminister cate chism in his left pocket."

The natives were trapped in the cave and were prepared to die. As the settlers and soldiers prepared to engage in battle, Witch Wonderful arrived, stood astride the Captain stating, "Shed no blood my friend, o you will live to regret it." She asked that they not slay the natives. She then requested time to speak to th natives, which was granted. The militiamen and settlers stood-down while Witch Wonderful went into th cave to secure an agreement of peace. The natives vowed they would not return to Lynn or Nahant and th militia agreed to the compromise, promising to spare them. Witch Wonderful had terminated a grievou battle before it commenced!

A procession across the sand bar to Lynn ensued with the natives leading as the captain and his lieu tenants and Witch Wonderful followed, while the remainder of the militia and settlers marched at the rear A great celebration was held that evening in Lynn in honor of Witch Wonderful and the comradeship o the native warriors. At the end of the celebration she made a private, grave statement, that she had bu two weeks more to live. On the following morning, multitudes of people arrived at High Rock to witnes

nd cheer the procession of native canoes leaving Saugus and heading toward Boston Bay and the south
nore.

Before going back to Salem, Witch Wonderful confided to the Elders of Lynn and the Captain of Militia
hat she was under all-powerful native protection for her many abilities to envision the future and find lost
rticles and for her desire to foster peace. Witch Wonderful later returned to her hut on the Salem shoreline
nd, true to her vision, two weeks later she was found deceased. The people of Lynn were grateful for her
ntervention of a massacre, and she was brought to Nahant with due ceremony and buried in the earth
verlooking the entrance to Swallow Cave where she enacted her peacemaking.

People claimed to have seen the ghost of Witch Wonderful walking on the rocky shoreline or in the cave
ollowing her interment, though there have been no documented sightings since the early 1800s.

An extremely rare image of Swallow Cave from seawards, c. 1900. *GWB*

Interior view of Swallow Cave looking outward, c. 2015. *ABG*

The jagged entrance to Swallow Cave,
with Madame Emily Cook-Pauli, c. 2019. *SEC*

Swallow Cave
under heavy seas,
c. 2018. *HAC*

Artist's conception of Witch Wonderful,
from a historic print. *GWB*

Chapter Nine

Flying Saucers

Enter the sky mysteries... There have been a number of "flying saucer," "flying disc," or "unidentified flying object" sightings over Lynn, Nahant, and the greater Boston area. Lights in the sky during periods of darkness have been common for many years, but mostly ignored. Unidentified Flying Object sightings were spoken of by the natives to the first explorers and settlers in Boston.

In 1639, Governor John Winthrop documented a secondhand sighting or observation from Mr. James Everell. On the early evening of March 1, 1639, Mr. Everell and comrades were rowing a small boat in the Muddy River when his attention was brought to a "great light" in the sky.

The Governor entered into his journal that the light, "when it stood still, it flamed up, and was about three yards square; when it ran, it was contracted into the figure of a swine: it ran as swift as an arrow towards Charlton [Charlestown], and so up and down about two or three hours." Governor Winthrop regarded Mr. Everell a "sober and discrete man," and made note that while watching this most unusual phenomenon they found themselves one mile upstream with absolutely no memory of how they arrived there. Lights in the sky were observed for many years but attributed to meteors or mythical Paganistic creatures. The thought of manned aerial flights was pure fantasy and only spoken in relation of white or dark angels.

The beginning of intense interest in flying saucers commenced in 1949 and continued through the 1950s when Boston and Lynn newspaper headlines broadcast news and photographs of the infamous Lubbock Lights in Texas. On August 30, 1951, the Lubbock Lights, as they came to be known, were witnessed by countless observers and photographed by Carl Hart, Jr., a 19 year old man. The photograph indicates an object in a "V" form with 15 or more bluish-green lights on the trailing edge. They appeared at 9:20 p.m., and reappeared an hour later. Witnesses stated that the object(s) moved slowly and very quietly. Sightings of the blue-green

Headlines of the <u>Boston American</u> newspaper, Monday, July 7th, 1947. *GWB*

lights were now constant in the Texas area. The observers had witnessed something fantastic and perhaps other-worldly.

The lights glided over Lubbock, other nearby small towns and along highways. Witnesses varied on the amount of light displayed while some remarked that they were the exhaust of jet engines and not lights which glowed by themselves. In evening hours, farmers, children, and families relaxing on their porches, saw the lights quickly and quietly gliding over homes and yards. One woman said that it was a large object, "like a huge aircraft, minus its body."

Following a late September investigation by United States Air Force Intelligence, hundreds of witnesses came forth. Under the direction of Captain Edward Ruppelt, *Project Blue Book* investigated and compiled all sighting incidents. The Lubbock Lights were sighted and documented twelve more times, and thus began the "flying saucer" phenomenon in the United States. Much reasoning was formed about the strange sightings, which included birds reflecting light from street lights, reflections on water appearing in the night sky, meteors, and weather analyzing instruments, such as reflective silver balloons.

Testimony of witnesses in and near Lubbock, Texas, gave accurate and some obscure descriptions of the lights, but they all confirmed that it was an experience none of them would ever forget.

New England also had its share of flying saucer sightings. On July 16th, 1952, a formation of four flying aucers was photographed at the United States Coast Guard Air Station in Salem, Massachusetts. The incident was widely reported by many newspapers, including the The Courier Express, from Buffalo, New York, dated August 2nd, 1952.

The photograph was released by the Salem Coast Guard Air Station headquarters for general knowledge and because of the widespread interest in the subject. The image was taken at 9:35 a.m. and showed a formation of four large and bright flying saucers in a "V" formation. The Coast Guardsman that took the photographs, Seaman Shell R. Alpert, was the facility photographer and used a Bush Pressman Camera. He stated that the appearance was that of a quick flash and, "I actually could not say it was anything; it could have been reflections from passing

Seaman Shell R. Alpert, U. S. C. G, Salem Station, with camera and photograph. *CGD*

cars or from the ocean." Coast Guardsman Alpert remarked that he initially saw several brilliant lights through his photograph laboratory window. He watched the lights moving slowly and wavering, "only to have them dim down by the time he had focused his camera."

Seaman Alpert called for a fellow Coast Guardsman, Seaman Thomas Flaherty, and as they were commenting on the waning lights, they grew brilliant once more and a series of photographs were quickly captured. "He said an instant later there was a 'momentary flash' and the lights disappeared." Alpert stated that he could not identify the lights or the sighting whether they were "objects or aircraft; (they were) merely some manner of lights."

Coast Guard authorities at Salem and Boston commented that "it had no opinion as to the cause or source" of the "objects" and classified them as "unidentified air phenomena." News reporter inquiries with other nearby military sources that suggested the Navy may have been firing antiaircraft guns or flare guns proved to be without bearing; the Air Force disclaimed any activity in the immediate Salem or offshore area as well, while the Army referred all inquiries to the local Public Information Office at Boston Army Base which gave no further information of any use.

Following intense investigation by Naval and Air Force Intelligence agencies, the images were initially thought to have been a hoax. Eleven years later they were reexamined and determined as reflections on window glass. They remain in Air Force Intelligence holdings, and remain officially as unidentified. At varying times throughout the investigations, the military designated the Unidentified Flying Objects case as either unusual occurrences or unconventional aircraft with no further information or specific examples.

Less than a week later, at 2 a.m. on the 22nd of July, the United States Coast Guard Station at Nahant documented what was thought to have been two unidentified flying objects. On duty that morning was Seaman Henry Arnpriester who provided a telephone interview with the *Lynn Telegram-News*, which appeared in Issue 23 in July of 1952. Coast Guardsman Arnpriester observed two bright discs, and stated,

> "...at 2:15 this morning I saw two strange objects which were certainly something new. I had never seen anything like them before. They appeared to be about five feet in diameter and were a light, hazy blue. I first saw them coming in from the southeast at an altitude of about 2,000 feet. They were traveling at great speed and appeared to be only a few feet apart.
>
> "They circled low off Egg Rock, dropping down to an altitude of a few hundred feet, and then climbed rapidly again and sped off in the same southeast direction from which they had come."

Seaman Henry Ampriester stated he was positive that the objects he saw were not 'birds, planes or anything like that. If they were, he said, he would have reported them as such." The Coast Guardsman continued: "I never believed any of those stories I've read about flying discs. I always thought the people who saw them were just imagining things. I'm convinced now there is something to those flying disc stories."

One particularly interesting flying saucer tale from Nahant harks back to November, 1959. A Lynn English High School Junior, Gerald W. Butler (the author) and a Sophomore, Francis Wangler, Jr., took photographs of a low-flying Unidentified Flying Object over a United States Army Air Defense Command missile tracking and control site at Bayley's Hill. The disc was photographed over the Administration Building and the main entrance to the facility. The Newspaper article was printed in a November 1959 issue of *The Lynn Daily Item*:

**Daylight capture of flying saucers at U. S. Coast Guard Station at
Salem, Massachusetts, c. 1952.** *CDG*

"FLYING OBJECT SPOTTED - Two Nahant boys photographed what they thought was a flying saucer
t noon on Saturday near Bass Point, Nahant. The unidentified object hovered over the bay between two
earby NIKE installations and the two boys managed to snap two photos of it before it disappeared.

Claiming to be the first to photograph a "flying saucer" in Greater Lynn are Frank Wangler of 63 Tri-
mountain Road and Gerald Butler of 12 Colby Way, both of Nahant. A check with U. S. ARMY and U. S.
AIR FORCE officials today indicated that the object was not - alas - a 'flying saucer' but a weather analyzing
nstrument, one of many frequently released to secure data."

Aside from seeming to rebuke their claim, the article delighted the two photographers, but the published newspaper article was not received well by their parents. Happily, the article was quickly forgotten, and th incident faded.

In reality, the flying saucer was not a weather analyzing instrument as the military had so confidentl and reassuringly claimed...but rather, a wooden model concocted and built by the author. It was painte silver. By means of a small length of thread and a stick it was photographed as if hovering over the activ control site. Of interest, the photograph was taken during the summer months, while the article was pul lished in November, when the trees were bare and the grass was dormant, in contrast pointed out by no on to the foliage in the photograph.

The Department of Defense (DOD) recently reestablished guidelines for pilots and observers that hav witnessed encounters with Unidentified Flying Objects. Accordingly, the United States Navy has create guidelines for pilots, observers and military personnel as there has been a surge of "intrusions" by unknow and highly advanced "objects" on Navy carrier strike forces and groups.

In December 2017, The Department of Defense admitted to having a special investigative branch calle

Nahant Coast Guard Station showing equipment and vehicles during the 1950s. *ABG*

A "Flying Saucer" over the missile control facility (IFC Area) at Nahant, Massachhusetts. *GWB*

the Advanced Aerospace Threat Identification Program (AATIP). The unit was in operation from 2007 through 2012.

Many flying saucer reports have been quite brief with little or no descriptions. At midnight, on August 30, 2017, an unidentified flying object was observed for three minutes and 12 seconds over the City of Lynn. Nothing else was documented or recorded of the incident. The last recorded Flying Saucer near and over Nahant was viewed on March 11th, 2018 at 7:25 in the evening.

A number of witnesses described it as an oval object, illuminated by three pulsing lights which turned transparent and quickly disappeared. The flying object was visible for one minute. The same sort of official sources that claimed, and subsequently dismissed, the author's fabrication decades prior indicated that this object was merely the result of swamp gas.

The author adds candidly, "It amazes me that Flying Saucers, Flying Discs, or Unidentified Flying Objects always have their landing or navigation lights on at night. For a foreign entity to be so advanced as to travel through space, and perhaps time as well, and to be so courteous as to identify themselves in our nighttime skies, is extremely commendable."

Chapter Ten

The Great Outbreak of 1692

Enter Misses Parris and Williams... It began in the late 1600s, with two young girls, Miss Elizabeth Parris, aged 11, and Miss Abigail Williams, aged 9, who, out of boredom, stated that they were possessed by the Devill through local witches. Accusations ensued, then panic, then hysteria rapidly spread throughout Salem Village and eventually led to accusations involving more than 200 local citizens. The hysteria followed closely to the pattern of early European Paganistic "witch hunts" of the 1300s.

When suspected of witchcraft, citizens were brought to Salem for hearings. If they were formerly accused by the Magistrate, they were brought to a prison and chained to the prison walls in the prison's sub-basement, or "witch jail." Accused witches were kept separate from all other prisoners so as not to affect or taint them through witchcraft. The jail cells were absolutely horrendous. They were constantly dark, cold, and wet, with all manner of insects and rats running about freely. The masonry walls were of stone and constantly ran with water and condensation while the floors were dirt and covered with feces and urine.

Executions

There are four execution dates that nineteen women and men were taken to Proctor's Ledge to suffer by hanging from a tree until dead. Additionally, a 71 year old man was "pressed" to death at an unknown date as the result of related accusations. The dates and certainly falsely accused people were:

June 10, 1692, Bridget Bishop.
July 19, 1692, Sarah Good, Rebecca Nurse, Susannah Martin, Elizabeth Howe and Sarah Wildes.

August 19, 1692, Martha Carrier, John Willard, Reverend George Burroughs, George Jacobs Sr. and John Proctor.

September 22, 1692, Mary Eastey, Martha Corey, Ann Pudeator, Samuel Wardwell, Mary Parker, Alice Parker, Wilmot Redd and Margaret Scott.

Date Unknown, Mr. Giles Corey, 71 years old, was executed by being "pressed" by stones, his punishment for refusing to enter either an innocent or guilty plea to the magistrate.

Mr. Giles Cory, 71 years of age, in process of being "pressed." From an old print. *PUB*

Lydia Dustin, Ann Foster, Sarah Osborne and Roger Toothaker died in prison waiting for their execution dates. Due to the judgments against them they were not allowed proper Christian burials and their corpses were placed in unmarked shallow graves, or in some instances, wedged into rock crevices. Families reclaimed the bodies of Rebecca Nurse, John Proctor and George Jacobs under the cover of night, and gave them proper Christian burials on family-owned properties.

During their incarcerations, the accused witches were constantly and relentlessly forced to undergo minute physical examinations of their bodies. The female prisoners, mostly mature or elderly, were disrobed before a group of men who acted as self-appointed investigators and who intensely scrutinized them for odd or suspicious markings. Privacy and modesty were nonexistent for the female prisoners. Simultaneously, the females were humiliated by being jabbed, cut, pricked, and prodded in front of witnesses.

The appointed examiners were searching for evidence that the accused was indeed a witch. The supposed evidence they sought included deformations or special markings thought to be of supernatural origin. This included severe inspections of "a teat from which the witch's familiar was believed to have nursed." Many times the investigators found birthmarks that were used as evidence of the Devill's markings.

Each day of imprisonment, women's breasts were carefully inspected multiple times seeking indications of breastfeeding and lactation, regardless of their ages, under suspicion they could, or had been, nursing demons. Each inspection was documented and publicly debated in the courtroom.

In his book on Salem witchcraft, With an Account of Salem Village and a History of Opinions on Witchcraft and Kindred Spirits, the author Mr. Charles W. Upham describes his disgust over this vile and inhumane treatment of the accused:

Artist's ink rendition of a Salem witch trial, by Freeland A. Carter. *PUB*

"The mind loathes the thought of handling in this way refined and sensitive females of matronly character, or persons of either sex, with infirmities of body rendered sacred by years. The results of the examinations were reduced to written reports, going into details, and, among other evidences in the trials, spread before the court and jury."

In 1711, a bill pardoning the victims was passed that granted monetary restitution to the surviving victims and their families. Unfortunately, hundreds of people's lives had been stained and corrupted by the Salem "witch hunts" and subsequent trials. Twenty four innocent people died for supposed involvement in dark magick. Incredibly, suspicions of witchcraft also caused two dogs to be executed.

Disregarding common folklore, none of the accused "witches" tried in Salem or locally were burned at the stake, as this was reserved mostly for members of the military and militia.

There was no documentation of witchcraft practiced in Nahant during the 1600s, or later, for that matter, though it was most concerning elsewhere and did have an impact on the township. The slightest whim or dislike for another could set in motion a terrifying ordeal. Many of the accusers tried to gain the elimi-

The first accused witch, M. Bridget Bishop, was hanged on June 10, 1692. *GWB*

nation of a competitor by false statements At the height of the *Great Outbreak of 1692* most of the accused were brought to trial without having done anything toward or against anyone. The actual investigative process was elaborate, and undertaken or terminated largely at the mercy of the accuser.

Some accused individuals were mentally or physically challenged. Others, possibly including accusers, may have been unwittingly under the influence of ergot, a fungus that infects improperly stored rye and from which LSD can be derived. The ordeal showcased some of the worst aspects of humanity.

In his book, *Annals of Witchcraft in New England,* published in 1869, Mr. Samuel G Drake illuminates that many of the magistrates were of such character in investigating and delivering sentences, that they should rightly have been the ones to receive such sentences. A lawyer, having grown weary of obviously vindictive people, eloquently stated, "Besides, we are told by an able Lawyer of that time (Sir Robert Filmer) that 'the Devil could not be lawfully summoned' to bring his book into Court."

It was a frightening period of New England history, finally ended through the judicious application of logic, and possibly, by running out of ergot-spoiled rye.

The basic construction and application of the process to accuse and sentence a person of witchcraft followed this established pattern:

1. *The afflicted person makes a complaint to the Magistrate about a suspected witch. The complaint is sometimes made through a third person.*
2. *The Magistrate issues a warrant for the arrest of the accused person.*

3. *The accused person is taken into custody and examined by two or more Magistrates. If, after listening to testimony, the Magistrate believes that the accused person is probably guilty, the accused is sent to jail for possible reexamination and to await trial.*

4. *The case is presented to the Grand Jury. Depositions relating to the guilt or innocence of the accused are entered into evidence.*

5. *If the accused is indicted by the Grand Jury, he or she is tried before the Court of Oyer and Terminer. A jury, instructed by the Court, decides the defendant's guilt.*

6. *The convicted defendant receives his or her sentence from the Court. In each case at Salem, the convicted defendant was sentenced to be hanged on a specified date.*

7. *The Sheriff and his deputies carry out the sentence of death on the specified date.*

Shortly thereafter, new Magistrates and other lawful enforcers were placed by the King and the New England communities slowly returned to their normalcy.

Then, almost as soon as it had begun, the hysteria that swept through Puritan Massachusetts ended.

Exhaustive research has recently proven that the unfortunate victims of the Great Outbreak of 1692 were not hung at Gallow's Hill, rather, at nearby Proctor's Ledge. Recently installed, a tastefully curved, granite apron-style wall displays the names of the unfortunate souls hung and pressed during the outbreak. The monument is well tended by the City of Salem and numerous volunteers.

A cell of "the Salem witch dungeon." Image c. 1935.

Chapter Eleven

Myths and Rhymes & the Maiden in the Mist

Enter the mist... During the Spanish-American War, or War of 1898 as it is increasingly recognized, areas on the tip and landward side of East Point were selected for temporarily military signaling and other purposes. Sentinels were posted on both cliff and land areas patrolling the periphery of the strategic miltary site. The two appointed land routes began at Bass Beach, now known as Forty Steps Beach, through Canoe Beach, not far from the entrance to East Point. The second land route included all of Swallow Cave Road and then wound back to the entrance at East Point.

When the monotonous two hour tour of duty ended, the sentinels relaxed and rested until their next patrol. One fateful day, the sentinel charged with patrolling the Canoe and Bass Beach area tried relaxing but found he was not tired and took a short walk to what is now known as Forty Steps. The summer night had grown cool and a light fog began to roll in off the Atlantic Ocean.

As it was before midnight, he noticed a form in the light mist and darkness. Naturally he became apprehensive but as he approached, the form materialized into a young woman with a shawl draped over her head and shoulders. He was greatly surprised to see anyone at that late hour but greatly relieved the form did not materialize into something more obviously threatening.

Upon passing, she gave him a pleasant nod and continued down Nahant Road until she disappeared in the swirls of fog. The soldier continued on his relaxing walk and gave little thought to the chance meeting.

The soldier was assigned the same post on the following night. As he neared Swallow Cave Road he saw what appeared to be the same woman emerging from the mist once again. They both passed each other and he could not help to notice that she was, indeed, a very beautiful young lady.

An Army sentinel of 1898. *GWB*

She smiled and spoke to him saying that she would meet him again, and once again, was enveloped in mist and continued walking into the fog. The sentinel completed his tour of duty, and soon after went for another walk, hoping to see the mysterious woman. Unfortunately, he did not.

Nights followed and the sentinel did not see or meet the young lady. On a Thursday afternoon of that week, a small fishing sailing craft foundered in heavy seas and began to sink off East Point. The sea quickly pushed the sinking craft toward the jagged rocks off Spouting Horn. A life-saving surfboat was summoned from the Nahant Humane Society of Massachusetts Life Saving Station by the Army sentinels. At that time, the rudimentary life saving station was located near the original wharf off Vernon Street, between Joseph's Beach and Bathing Beach.

Recognized officially as *Station Number 12 of the United States Life Saving Station at Nahant*, the facility was not completed until 1900. However, a crew of six and a surfboat were stationed at the site beforehand in the event of storms and emergencies.

Unfortunately, by the time the surfmen rowed around East Point, the fishing boat had mostly sunk with only a small portion of the deck above water. Clinging to the debris were two men and a young woman who was holding what appeared to be a small child in one arm.

On shore, most of the small military garrison from East Point had been alerted and gathered near Castle Rock with thought of aiding the distressed vessel and passengers. The soldier in question managed to obtain a set of binoculars from a junior officer to observe the tragedy unfolding.

When the surfboat neared the wreck, the young woman threw the baby to a rowman on the boat. He caught the child and the woman attempted to jump from the sinking craft into the rescue boat. Unfortunately, she misjudged her timing, and fell between the debris and the surfboat.

Before any of the surfmen could reach her she was pulled down by the churning sea and propelled out toward Egg Rock. She was quickly swept away and her lifeless form was never recovered. As the soldier or

Castle Rock, shown under a tranquil setting, with Bird's Egg Rock beyond, c. 1900. *LPL*

he shore took the binoculars away rom his eyes, he realized that she vas the young woman he had seen n the fog. The two fishermen were rought to the military post and alowed to dry out and rest. The next norning they departed East Point vhile no further information about he young lady, baby or fishermen vas recorded.

Nautical Themes

The Weather

Present day weather is forecast using satellites, computers, and ar-reaching, sophisticated electronc systems. Long before the advent of these complex devices, there were n place rhymes that every grammar chool child memorized to predict he weather. In the early 1700s, and omewhat beyond, the following hymes existed:

"Rain before seven,
  Clear before 'leven.
Red in the morning,
  Sailors take warning;
Red at night,

A tranquil beginning to a lobsterman's day. *GWB*

A Supermoon over Boston Harbor from atop Bayley's Hill. Original photograph by Alanna Butler-Guptill, modified and redrawn by author.
GWB

Nahauntus

> Sailors delight.
> Rainbow in the morning,
>   Sailors take warning.
> Rainbow at night,
>   Sailors delight;
> Rainbow at noon,
>   Rain very soon.

A new stanza evolved during the 1850s:

> When the wind is to the north,   When the wind is to the south,
> The fisherman he goes not forth; It blows the bait in the fish's mouth
> When the wind is to the east,   When the wind is to the west,
> 'Tis neither good for man   Then 'tis at the very best.
>   nor beast,

During the late 1800s, the verse was shortened once again:

> Wind from the east, bad for man and for beast;
>   Wind from the south, is too hot for them both;
> Wind from the north, is of very little worth;
>   Wind from the west, is the softest and the best.

The modern weather rhyme is but two lines:

> Red sky at night - sailor's delight
>   Red sky in morning - sailor take warning.

Crows

Witchcraft is not all considered evil, as "Won-erful, the Witch" proved in the account of Swal-ow Cave. Witchcraft used many forms and ani-nals of Mother Earth, to include cats, crows and erpents. Of them all, the crow has a very special ignificance by both Wicca and other recognized Covens of Witches. There are many ancient fables nd rhymes concerning crows, each of which gen-rally concerned wisdom in and of the future.

The Black Crow, harbinger of messages. GWB

Counting Crows:

One Crow — bad luck, loss, death, unpleasant catastrophic change
Two Crows — Good luck, and a major change for the better, joy
Three Crows — A wedding or celebration, or the birth of a girl
Four Crows — A birth, particularly of a boy, a new beginning
Five Crows — Money coming in, good business
Six Crows — Major money change, could mean loss or gain
Seven Crows — A secret, a mystery, or a curse
Eight Crows — A life altering experience, usually positive
Nine Crows — Love, positive recognition
Ten Crows — A complete turnaround in luck
Eleven Crows — News, surprise, secrets hidden or revealed
Twelve Crows — Also good luck, completion, fulfillment
Thirteen Crows — Completion, the end of a situation

Another modern rendition:

One for sorrow, two for mirth.
  Three for a wedding, and four for a birth.
Five for silver, six for gold.
  Seven for a secret... not to be told.

More directly:

One crow sorrow, Two crows mirth,
  three crows a wedding, four crows a birth,
five brings silver, six takes wealth,
  seven crows a secret, I can't tell.

The <u>Dictionary of Superstitions</u> by Oxford University Press published this version in 1992:

One for sorrow,   *five for rich,*
two for mirth,   *six for poor,*
three for a wedding,   *Seven for a witch,*
four for birth,   *I can tell you no more.*

Lilium flowers with the Magic Moon. Artwork by Itskatjas

Chapter Twelve

Sirens of the Sea

Enter the Mermaid... During the early 1600s, coastal natives informed the early explorers and initial settlers of the beautiful Mermaids and the protective Mermen that frequented the rocks and cliffs of Nahantus.

A mermaid is a legendary aquatic creature with the head and upper form of a beautiful young woman while the lower portion is that of a fish. They are an essential figure of Greek, Egyptian, Celtic, Japanese, and Inuit traditions. Legends of mermaids began when man first sailed the oceans. A short, but meaningful poem, composed by A.M. Galdorcraeft, describes these sirens of the sea:

Sisters of the tide are we,
  Bound by sand, and salt, and sea.
Selkie, mermaid, siren daughters,
  Priestesses of the holy waters.

The first recorded sightings appeared in ancient Assyria, when the goddess *Atargatis* transposed her female form into a mermaid in shame for accidentally killing her human lover. At present, the Hindus place a mermaid goddess in the highest esteem.

Sailors have since told countless tales of the elusive beckoning mermaids, some of whom are said to be evil, while others appeared kind. Mermaids have been said to lure ships to their destruction by singing their siren calls or causing tidal waves and storms to induce drownings.

Other legends describe the mermaid more sympathetically, and in many instances, enticingly, and as giving gifts or imparting sensual dreams. In some instances, lonely seafaring men have fallen in love with

**A mermaid resting on a pebble beach,
arranging her hair.** *GWB*

mermaids, generally with disastrous results.

The mermaid has generally been portrayed as an exceptionally beautiful young woman with long, thic
hair, constantly preening atop cliffs overlooking the sea. Their means of coming ashore from the deep is said
to be by way of rock formations known as "Mermaid's Staircases," of which Nahant has many.

The staircases begin at the waters' edge and continue up natural inclines until attaining a plateau o
sufficient height for mermaids to relax and sun themselves and observe passing ships.

The Sirens of Greek mythology have greatly influenced tales and stories of mermaids. Historical doc
umentation even include mermaid sightings recorded by Christopher Columbus, when he claimed to se
three at one time during his Caribbean exploits.

Later investigations indicated that the sightings by mariners may have been attributed to manatees and
other similar aquatic mammals on the surface and near land. Whether glimpsed through inebriation, or th

A superb example of a "Mermaid's Staircase" plainly viewed at the tip of East Point, Nahant. *ABG*

distorting prism of lonely sailors' hope, is unclear.

The worlds of literature and visuals arts have featured mermaids for generations. Mermaids remain a popular subject for both children and adults. The most famous mermaid tale is likely *The Little Mermaid,* published in 1836, by Hans Christian Andersen...albeit modern adaptations of the characters and story depart greatly from the ghastlier elements of the original work.

Later, entire operas, books, films, comic books, and all manner of toys and items have featured mermaids. Mermaids even feature in the classic *One Thousand and One Nights,* where they are described reverentially and quite eloquently. The mermaid's sea companion is the merman, although sightings and knowledge concerning mermen is somewhat limited and less common than mermaids. While there is no photographic proof of their existence, their popularity endures in art, culture, and the lore of the sea.

About the Author

Gerald W. Butler, a Captain in the Massachusetts State Guard, was the former curator at Forts Warren and Independence, Boston Harbor and Fort Rodman, New Bedford. He has published *Military Annals of Nahant, Military History of the Cape Cod Canal, Military History of Boston's Harbor Islands, The Guns of Boston Harbor, Fort Warren: The Key to Boston Harbor, Naval Secrets of Nahant, Shemya - America's Cold war Sentinel, Concrete monoliths, Fort Ruckman Through Time, Eastpont Through Time,* and *Sails and Rails* (*f*/64 Publishing). He lectures and serves as a consultant to military museums and state parks, was the former historian for U.S. Navy mine units, and his illustrations of seacoast fortifications are published worldwide.

Also Available
from f/64 Publishing

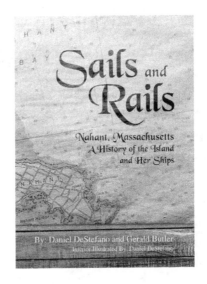

ISBN: 978-0-9831858-4-0
$24.95

ISBN: 978-0-9831858-3-3
$14.95

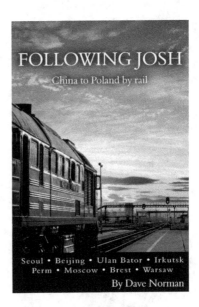

ISBN: 978-0-9831858-1-9
$15.95

CPSIA information can be obtained
at www.ICGtesting.com
Printed in the USA
BVHW011953031019
560171BV00006B/17/P